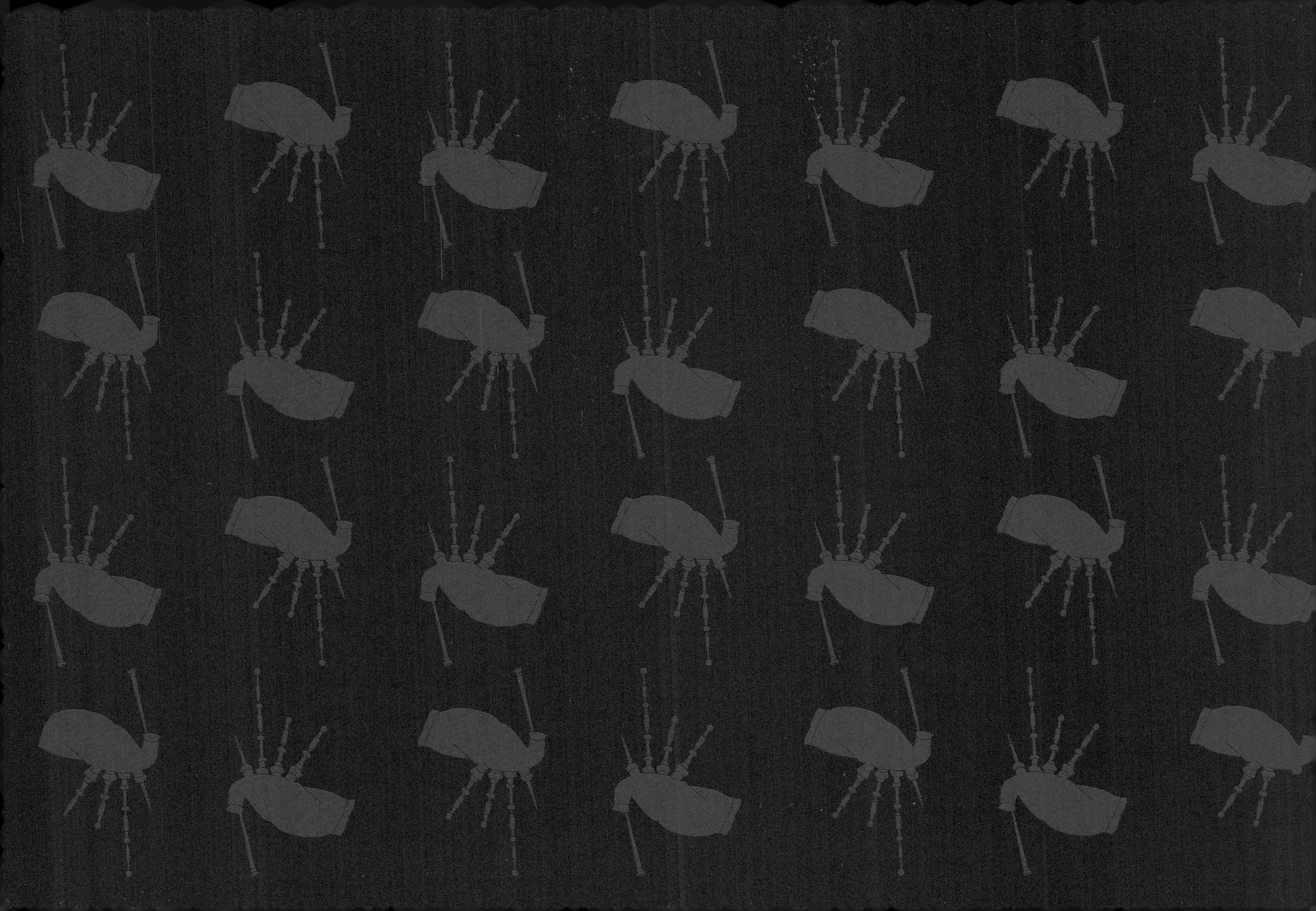

AXEL M. MOSLER

SCOTLAND PANORAMA

Text by Ralf Gantzhorn

EDITIONPANORAMA

SCHOTTLAND

„Nie sah ich Einsameres. Der Bühnenraum eines Riesentheaters, dessen Perspektive durch allerhand Seitenkulissen ins Unendliche zu wachsen scheint“, schrieb einst Theodor Fontane in seinem Klassiker „Jenseits des Tweed.“ Der märkische Dichter erlebt die herbe Schönheit, die Weite und das Licht der schottischen Highlands als wahren Rausch.

Ja, Schottland ist anders. „So near – so different“ ließ die Fremdenverkehrszentrale vor wenigen Jahren titeln und dies gilt nicht nur für die Landschaft. So wird kaum ein Besucher Schottlands umhin können, allerorten Geschichte und Geschichten zu begegnen – worauf die Schotten überaus stolz sind. Es gibt kaum ein anderes Land, dessen Bewohner ihre nationale Identität so stark aus ihrer Historie herleiten. In Schottland wimmelt es nur so von legendären Gestalten, deren Freiheitswille, Humor und Widersprüchlichkeit die schottische Mentalität widerspiegeln. Dabei hat Schottland nur fünf Millionen Einwohner. Aber diese haben dem Rest der Welt erfolgreich vermittelt, was es heißt, ein Schotte zu sein. Kilt und Dudelsack, Nessie und Whisky werden auch bei uns von Kindesalter an mit dieser Gegend am Rande Europas assoziiert.

Das kleine Land umfasst den nördlichen Teil der britischen Inseln. Von einer Linie aus, die man zwischen dem Solway Firth im Westen und der Mündung des Tweed im Osten ziehen kann, beginnt Kaledonien, „bewaldetes Land“, wie es einst von den Römern genannt wurde. Vom Wald ist

SCOTLAND

“Never did I see anywhere more lonely. The stage area of a gigantic theatre, whose perspectives seem to extend beyond the wings into infinity”, once wrote the Brandenburg author Theodor Fontane in his classic “Beyond the Tweed.” The Brandenburg author was experiencing the stark beauty, the expansiveness and the light of the Scottish highlands as a genuine intoxication.

Yes, Scotland is different. “So near – so different” ran the slogan of the Scottish Tourist Board a few years ago, and this applies not only to the landscape. Hardly any visitor to Scotland can avoid coming across all sorts of history and stories – of which the Scots are very proud. There is hardly any other country whose inhabitants derive their national identity so much from their history. Scotland abounds in legendary figures whose yearning for freedom, humour and contradiction reflect the Scottish mentality. Although Scotland has a population of only 5 million, the Scots have succeeded in conveying to the rest of the world what it means to be a Scot. Kilts and bagpipes, Nessie and whisky are associated by us from early childhood with this region on the outer edge of Europe.

This small country occupies the northern part of the British Isles. Caledonia, the “wooded country”, as it was once called by the Romans, begins from a line drawn between the Solway Firth in the west and the mouth of the Tweed in the east. Little now remains of the forests which once covered the land, for they were systematically felled to feed the

ECOSSE

« Je n'ai jamais rien vu de plus solitaire. Comme la scène d'un immense théâtre dont les coulisses latérales semblent dérouler la perspective à l'infini », a écrit autrefois le poète Theodor Fontane, originaire de la marche de Brandebourg, dans son œuvre classique « Jenseits des Tweed ». Il découvre une véritable ivresse dans la beauté austère, les vastes immensités et la lumière des Highlands écossais.

C'est vrai, l'Ecosse est différente des autres pays. Il y a quelques années, les offices de tourisme écossais promouvaient son image avec le slogan « So near – so different » et cela ne s'appliquait pas uniquement au paysage. L'histoire mais aussi les histoires sont partout présentes en Ecosse – ce dont les Ecossais sont particulièrement fiers. Rares sont les pays dont les habitants tirent si fortement leur identité de leur histoire. L'Ecosse fourmille de personnages légendaires dont l'amour de la liberté, l'humour et les contradictions reflètent la mentalité écossaise. Le pays ne compte pourtant que cinq millions d'habitants mais ceux-ci ont su montrer au reste du monde ce que c'est qu'être écossais. Depuis notre enfance, l'Ecosse, à la périphérie de l'Europe, c'est pour nous le kilt, la cornemuse, le monstre du Loch Ness et le whisky.

Ce petit pays englobe la partie nord des Iles Britanniques. Depuis une ligne que l'on peut tracer entre le Solway Firth à l'ouest et l'estuaire de la Tweed à l'est, la Calédonie « pays boisé » ainsi que l'avaient baptisée les Romains jadis, commence. Il ne reste toutefois pratiquement rien de cette

ESCOCIA

"Nunca había visto nada tan solitario. El escenario de un gigantesco teatro cuya perspectiva parece perderse en el infinito que recrean sus variados bastidores laterales". Así describía sus sentimientos el poeta alemán Theodor Fontane en su obra clásica "Más allá del Tweed." El escritor, oriundo de la Marca de Brandemburgo, experimentó la vastedad y la luz de las Tierras Altas de Escocia –las famosas "Highlands"– casi como la belleza.

Sí, Escocia es diferente. Hace pocos años la Central británica de promoción del turismo eligió "Tan cerca y tan diferente" como lema de su campaña. Un eslogan que en esta región no sólo se puede aplicar al paisaje. Quien visita Escocia no puede evitar encontrarse a su paso historia e historias, algo que llena de orgullo a los escoceses. Hay pocos países en los que sus habitantes sientan tan profundamente que su historia constituye el sustento de su identidad nacional. En el pasado de Escocia abundan las figuras legendarias que reflejan el ansia de libertad, el humor y el carácter contradictorio de la mentalidad escocesa. Y eso que Escocia sólo tiene cinco millones de habitantes, pero que han sabido demostrarle al mundo qué significa ser un escocés. Prácticamente todos los europeos asocian desde niños el "kilt" –la famosa falda masculina–, la gaita, el monstruo "Nessie" y el whisky con esta región al borde de Europa.

Este pequeño país abarca el norte de las islas británicas. Al norte de una línea imaginaria que se podría trazar de oeste a este entre el "Solway Firth" y la desembocadura del río

SCOZIA

„Mai fui testimone di tanta solitudine. La scena di un enorme teatro, la cui prospettiva sembra estendersi all'infinito, attraverso numerose quinte laterali" scrisse un tempo il poeta della Marca Theodor Fontane nel suo classico „Viaggio attraverso la Scozia". La bellezza aspra, l'estensione e la luce delle Highlands scozzesi suscitarono nel poeta della Marca autentica ebbrezza.

È vero, la Scozia è diversa. „So near – so different" proclamava pochi anni fa l'ente per il turismo estero. Uno slogan calzante, che non vale solo per il paesaggio. Difficilmente il visitatore della Scozia potrà evitare d'imbattersi nella sua storia e nelle sue storie: di questo gli scozzesi sono estremamente fieri. Gli abitanti di nessun altro paese fanno derivare con tanto fervore la loro identità nazionale dalla loro storia. La Scozia brulica di figure leggendarie: la loro determinazione nel conquistare la libertà, il loro umore e il loro carattere contraddittorio rispecchiano la mentalità scozzese. Eppure la Scozia ha solo cinque milioni di abitanti che, tuttavia, sono riusciti a trasmettere in modo chiaro al resto del mondo cosa significhi essere scozzese. Ecco perché sin dalla nostra infanzia siamo abituati ad associare questa regione posta ai margini dell'Europa ai kilt, alle cornamuse, a Nessie e allo whisky.

Questo piccolo paese comprende la parte settentrionale delle Isole britanniche. La Caledonia, ovvero „la terra ricoperta di boschi", come i romani usavano chiamarla un tempo, si estende a nord della linea che collega Solway

allerdings nicht mehr viel übrig geblieben, denn er wurde im Rahmen eines ambitionierten Schiffbauprogramms seitens der natürlichen Feinde der Schotten – der Engländer – systematisch zerstört. Übrig geblieben ist eine Heide- und Moorlandschaft, die wir heute für typisch schottisch halten. Und eine Animosität zwischen Engländern und Schotten, die ebenfalls bis heute andauert und Teil der schottischen Identität ist. Bei Fußballbegegnungen wie etwa dem Europameisterschaftsspiel gegen England schwenken die Anhänger der Schotten, die Tartan Army, Fahnen mit der Zahl 1314. Was das bedeuten soll? 1314 ist die Jahreszahl des letzten überzeugenden Sieges der Schotten über die Engländer auf dem Schlachtfeld von Bannockburn.

Mit einer Fläche von 78 762 Quadratkilometern ist Schottland ungefähr so groß wie Österreich. Ganz im Süden, an der Grenze zu England, liegen die Southern Uplands. Sie bilden eine hügelige, vom Tourismus vergessene Region voller reizvoller Überraschungen. Ihre Schlagader ist der River Tweed, der am 840 Meter hohen Broad Law entspringt und durch eine von sanft rollenden Hügeln und grünen Tälern geprägte Kulturlandschaft nach rund 160 Kilometern in die Nordsee mündet. In seinem Einzugsbereich liegen die Überreste der Abbeys von Crossraguel, Melrose, Jedburgh und Dryburgh; große Kathedralen und Klöster, die vom einstigen Reichtum der Gegend zeugen, heute jedoch nur noch Ruinen sind. Zerstört wurden sie bereits im 16. Jahrhundert von – wem sonst – den Engländern. Erhalten blieben sie als Inbegriff der „romantischen Ruine" und Sir Walter Scott machte sie berühmt mit folgenden

ambitious ship-building programme of the natural enemies of the Scots – the English. What has remained is a landscape of heath and moorland, which is today considered typical of Scotland. And an animosity between the English and Scots which persists to the present day, and forms part of the Scottish identity. At football matches such as the European Championship game against England, the Scottish fans, the Tartan Army, wave flags emblazoned with the date 1314. What does this mean? 1314 was the year of the last decisive victory of the Scots over the English on the battlefield of Bannockburn.

With an area of 30,410 mi^2, Scotland is approximately the size of Austria. In the south, on the border with England, lie the Southern Uplands. They form a hilly region, which although largely overlooked by tourism is full of fascinating surprises. The main artery of the region is the River Tweed, which rises on the 2,756 ft. high Broad Law and flows for around 100 miles through a landscape of gently undulating hills and green valleys before entering the North Sea. Its catchment area contains the remains of Crossraguel, Melrose, Jedburgh and Dryburgh Abbeys; large cathedrals and monasteries which testify to the former wealth of the area, although today nothing more than ruins. Destroyed in the 16th Century by – who else but – the English. They remain preserved as the embodiment of "romantic ruins" and were made famous by Sir Walter Scott in the following lines: "If thou would'st view fair Melrose aright, go visit it by the pale moonlight; For the gay beams of lightsome day gild, but to flout, the ruins grey." To the extreme west of the Southern Uplands lies Galloway, a region which represents

forêt car elle a été systématiquement détruite par les ennemis naturels des Ecossais, les Anglais évidemment, dans le cadre d'un programme ambitieux de construction navale. Cette hécatombe a laissé derrière elle un paysage de bruyères et de tourbières qui est pour nous indissociable de l'Ecosse. Et une animosité entre les Anglais et les Ecossais, vivace encore de nos jours et qui est l'un des éléments de l'identité écossaise. Pendant des rencontres sportives, comme par exemple lors du match de la Coupe d'Europe de foot contre les Anglais, les Ecossais, l'armée tartane, agitaient des drapeaux avec le chiffre 1314. Pourquoi ce chiffre ? Tout simplement parce que 1314 est l'année de la dernière victoire écrasante des Ecossais sur les Anglais sur le champ de bataille de Bannockburn.

Avec une superficie de 78 762 m^2, l'Ecosse est à peu près de la taille de l'Autriche. Tout au sud, les Southern Uplands la séparent de l'Angleterre. Ces terres sont une région vallonnée délaissée par le tourisme mais regorgeant de trésors. L'artère principale de cette région est la rivière Tweed qui prend sa source dans la Broad Law à 840 m d'altitude puis se jette dans la Mer du Nord 160 km plus loin après avoir traversé un paysage culturel dominé par de douces collines et des vallées verdoyantes. On trouve à proximité les vestiges de Crossraguel, Melrose, Jedburgh et Dryburgh Abbey ; de grandes cathédrales et des monastères qui témoignent de l'ancienne prospérité de la région, mais dont il ne reste désormais que des ruines aujourd'hui. Ces édifices ont été détruits au XVIème siècle déjà, bien évidemment par les Anglais. Désormais l'incarnation de la «ruine romantique», Sir Walter Scott les a rendues célèbres

Tweed empieza Caledonia, "región de bosques", como la llamaron en su día los romanos. Desgraciadamente no resta mucho de los bosques, ya que fueron sistemáticamente destruidos por los enemigos naturales de los escoceses –los ingleses– en el marco de un ambicioso programa de construcción naval. En cambio quedó ese paisaje de landas y pantanos que hoy en día consideramos típico de Escocia. Y una acentuada animosidad entre escoceses e ingleses que sigue perdurando hasta la actualidad y que se ha convertido en parte de la identidad escocesa. En los encuentros futbolísticos como, por ejemplo, los partidos de la Eurocopa contra Inglaterra, los hinchas del equipo escocés –la "Tartan Army"– ondean banderas con la cifra 1314. ¿Se pregunta qué simboliza ese número? En el año 1314 los escoceses derrotaron por última vez de forma clara a los ingleses en la batalla de Bannockburn.

Con una superficie de 78.762 km^2, Escocia es aproximadamente igual de grande que Austria. En la parte más meridional, ya en la frontera con Inglaterra, se encuentra la región de las "Southern Uplands". Se trata de un paisaje cubierto de colinas y prácticamente olvidado por el turismo, pero pleno de excitantes sorpresas. La principal arteria de la región es el río Tweed que nace a 840 metros de altura, en el "Broad Law" y recorre sus 160 kilómetros de longitud a través de un paisaje agrario de suaves colinas y verdes valles hasta su desembocadura en el Mar del Norte. En su área de afluencia se encuentran los restos de Crossraguel, Melrose, Jedburgh y Dryburgh Abbey, grandes catedrales y monasterios que dan testimonio de la antigua riqueza de la región, pero que hoy son tan sólo ruinas. Fueron destruidos

Firth, a ovest, e la foce del fiume Tweed, a est. Di quelle foreste non è rimasto molto. Furono sistematicamente distrutte dagli inglesi, i nemici naturali degli scozzesi, nel corso di un ambizioso programma di costruzioni navali. È rimasto un paesaggio caratterizzato da brughiere e paludi dall'aspetto da noi oggi considerato tipicamente scozzese. Anche l'animosità tra gli inglesi e gli scozzesi, componente dell'identità di quest'ultimi, si è protratta fino a oggi. Durante gli incontri di calcio, come la partita del campionato europeo contro l'Inghilterra, i sostenitori degli scozzesi, riuniti nella Tartan Army, sventolano bandiere sulle quali compare il numero 1314. 1314 è l'anno a cui risale l'ultima convincente vittoria degli scozzesi sugli inglesi consumata sul campo di battaglia di Bannockburn.

Con una superficie di 78.762 chilometri quadrati, la Scozia è approssimativamente grande quanto l'Austria. All'estremo sud, al confine con l'Inghilterra, sorgono le Southern Uplands, una regione collinare dimenticata dai turisti, ricca d'affascinanti sorprese. Il fiume Tweed, l'arteria fluviale della regione, nasce a Broad Law a 840 metri di altezza. Dopo aver attraversato un paesaggio antropizzato contraddistinto da colline dolcemente arrotondate e valli verdeggianti sfocia, percorsi circa 160 chilometri, nel Mare del Nord. Nel suo bacino idrografico si trovano le rovine di Crossraguel, Melrose, Jedburgh e Dryburgh Abbey; oggi, di queste grandi cattedrali e abbazie, testimoni della trascorsa ricchezza della regione, rimangono solo i resti. Furono distrutte già nel XVI secolo dagli inglesi – da chi altri? Diventate simbolo delle „rovine romantiche", Sir

Zeilen: „Und willst Du des Zaubers sicher sein, so besuch Melrose beim Mondenschein; die goldene Sonne, das Tageslicht, sie passen zu seinen Trümmern nicht." Ganz im Westen der Southern Uplands liegt Galloway, eine Region, die einen kleinen schottischen Mikrokosmos für sich darstellt: Hochmoore, Waldstrecken, malerische Buchten und hügeliges Farmland wechseln in rascher Folge. Und durch den Golfstrom ist das Klima hier besonders mild, die Farbe Grün dominiert und man fühlt sich stark an das gegenüberliegende Irland erinnert. Parallel zur Grenze nach England verläuft der Hadrianswall. Die Römer bauten diese Mauer, um sich vor den Übergriffen der Barbaren aus dem Norden zu schützen. Aber Eroberer haben sich nur selten von Mauern zurückhalten lassen und im frühen Mittelalter konnten sie auch die Engländer nicht abschrecken. Damals wurden die Borders, wie die Region auch genannt wird, zum heftig umstrittenen Zankapfel zwischen Schottland und England. Einige Städte und Grafschaften wechselten dabei gleich mehrfach den Besitzer, mit manchmal noch heute kuriosen Folgen: So spielt der Fußballclub des kleinen Städtchens Berwick upon Tweed bei den Schotten mit, obwohl der Ort selbst seit rund 500 Jahren zu England gehört.

An die Southern Uplands schließen sich nördlich die Lowlands an, die auch Midland Valley genannt werden. Obwohl dieses Tal nur ein Fünftel des Landes einnimmt, wird es von fast drei Vierteln der Gesamtbevölkerung bewohnt. Hier liegen die beiden großen Stadtzentren des Landes, Glasgow und Edinburgh, zwei Metropolen, die gegensätzlicher kaum sein könnten. Edinburgh mit seiner

Scotland in microcosm: highland moor, stretches of forest, picturesque bays and rolling farmland alternate in rapid sequence. And due to the Gulf Stream, the climate here is particularly mild, the colour green dominates, and one is reminded strongly of Ireland only a few miles away across the sea. Parallel to the border with England runs Hadrian's Wall, which was built by the Romans to protect themselves against raids by the barbarians from the north. But conquerors rarely allow themselves to be kept out by walls, and in the early Middle Ages, these proved to be no deterrent to the English. At that time, the Borders, as the region is also called, became a hotly-disputed bone of contention between Scotland and England. Some towns and counties changed hands several times, with sometimes curious consequences today: the football club of the small town of Berwick upon Tweed for instance plays in the Scottish League, although the town itself has been part of England for around 500 years.

To the north of the Southern Uplands lie the Lowlands, which are also referred to as the Midland Valley. Although this valley covers only one fifth of the area of the country, it is home to almost three quarters of the total population. Here lie the two major conurbations of the country, Glasgow and Edinburgh, two metropolitan centres which could hardly be more opposite. With its historic old town, fortress and castle, Edinburgh is the beautiful capital city, a UNESCO world cultural heritage site, which is blessed with the largest, completely classically extended "new town" in Europe. This has elevated the city at the feet of the volcanic plug of Arthur's Seat into an architectural dream.

avec les lignes suivantes : « Et si tu veux t'assurer de la magie des lieux, contemple alors Melrose au clair de lune ; le soleil doré ou la lumière du jour ne convient pas à ses ruines. » Le Galloway, véritable petit microcosme de l'Ecosse, couvre l'extrême ouest des Southern Uplands : des tourbières de montagne, des bois, des baies pittoresques et des terres cultivables vallonnées se succèdent rapidement. Le climat, particulièrement doux ici grâce au Gulf Stream, le vert qui domine, tout cela rappelle l'Irlande, située juste en face. Le Mur d'Adrien construit par les Romains pour se protéger des attaques des barbares venant du Nord, les Pictes, s'étire parallèlement à la frontière avec l'Angleterre. Mais les conquérants se laissent rarement intimider par des fortifications et celles-ci n'ont pas non plus arrêté les Anglais au début du Moyen Age. Jadis, cette région des Borders a été une pomme de discorde âprement disputée entre l'Ecosse et l'Angleterre. Certaines villes et quelques comtés ont changé à plusieurs reprises de propriétaire avec, parfois, des conséquences encore étranges aujourd'hui : le club de foot de la petite ville de Berwick upon Tweed par exemple joue en Ecosse, bien que la ville proprement dite appartienne à la couronne d'Angleterre depuis environ 500 ans.

Les Lowlands, appelées aussi Midland Valley, occupent l'espace au nord des Southern Uplands. Bien que cette vallée ne couvre qu'un cinquième du pays, trois quarts de la population globale y vit, notamment dans les deux principales agglomérations écossaises, Glasgow et Edimbourg, deux métropoles fondamentalement différentes. Edimbourg avec sa cité historique, son château et son palais est une belle capitale, inscrite au patrimoine culturel de

ya en el siglo XVI por –¿quién si no?– los ingleses. Sus muros formaron el arquetipo de las "ruinas románticas" que tan famosas hizo Sir Walter Scott con las siguientes líneas: "Si quieres asegurarte de que el encanto tenga efecto, visita Melrose a la luz de la luna, ya que el dorado sol y la luz diurna no son propios del espíritu de sus ruinas". En el extremo occidental de las "Southern Uplands" se encuentra Galloway, una región que por sí misma forma un pequeño microcosmos escocés en la que se van sucediendo los pantanos altos, los bosques, las pintorescas bahías y las granjas entre colinas. En esta región bendecida por el suave clima que aporta la Corriente del Golfo domina tanto el color verde, que resulta natural acordarse de la vecina Irlanda. La Muralla de Adriano discurre aquí paralela a la frontera con Inglaterra. Los romanos la construyeron para protegerse de los ataques de los bárbaros del norte. Pero los conquistadores raramente se dejaron impresionar por los muros y por eso en la alta Edad Media tampoco supusieron ningún obstáculo para los ingleses. Fue entonces cuando los "Borders", como también se llama a esta región, se convirtió en la disputada manzana de la discordia entre Escocia e Inglaterra. Algunas ciudades y condados cambiaron varias veces de dueño, lo que dio lugar a curiosas consecuencias que a veces perduran hasta hoy. Por ejemplo el club de fútbol de la pequeña ciudad de Berwick upon Tweed juega de parte de los escoceses a pesar de que la localidad ya pertenece a Inglaterra desde hace 500 años.

Las "Southern Uplands" limitan al norte con las Tierras Bajas de Escocia, las "Lowlands", a las que también se denomina el "Midland Valley", el valle central. A pesar de

Walter Scott le rese celebri con queste parole: „Se vuoi essere sicuro della sua magia, devi visitare Melrose al chiaro di luna; il sole dorato e la luce del giorno non le si confanno." A ovest delle Southern Uplands sorge Galloway, un piccolo microcosmo scozzese separato da tutto il resto: alte torbiere, tratti di foresta, baie pittoresche e campagne collinose si alternano in rapida successione. La corrente del golfo rende il clima particolarmente mite; domina il colore verde, che ricorda molto la dirimpettaia Irlanda. Il Vallo di Adriano corre parallelo al confine con l'Inghilterra. I romani lo costruirono per difendersi dagli attacchi dei barbari provenienti dal nord. Il muro, tuttavia, non riuscì a tenere lontano né i conquistatori, né gli inglesi che arrivarono nel primo Medioevo. Allora i Borders, come viene anche chiamata la regione, divennero oggetto di un' intensa controversia tra Scozia e Inghilterra. Alcune città e contee cambiarono spesso appartenenza, talvolta con conseguenze curiose ancora oggi: la squadra di calcio della cittadina Berwick upon Tweed gioca con gli scozzesi, nonostante da circa 500 anni appartenga all'Inghilterra.

A nord delle Southern Uplands sorgono le Lowlands, chiamate anche Midland Valley. La valle è abitata da quasi tre quarti della popolazione complessiva, nonostante occupi solo un quinto del paese. Vi sorgono le città principali, Glasgow e Edimburgo, due metropoli che non potrebbero essere più diverse. Edimburgo, con il suo centro storico, il castello e la roccaforte, è la bella capitale, patrimonio culturale dell'umanità dell'UNESCO. La più grande „New Town" classicista d'Europa rende perfetta questa città ai piedi del vulcano estinto Arthur's Seat, trasformandola in

historischen Altstadt samt Schloss und Burg ist die schöne Hauptstadt, ein Weltkulturerbe der UNESCO, das mit der größten durchgängig klassizistisch ausgebauten „Neustadt" Europas gesegnet ist. Dies hat die Stadt zu Füßen des Vulkanstumpfes Arthur's Seat endgültig zu einem architektonischen Traum veredelt. „East-windy, west-endy", windig und versnobt, nennen das die Glasgower. Edinburgh sei zwar Capital, die Hauptstadt, aber Glasgow habe das Kapital, denn schon immer wurden in Glasgow Güter produziert und in Edinburgh nur konsumiert. Glasgows Slums und Fabriken stehen inmitten der Innenstadt, unweit des Clyde, auf einem Schachbrettmuster und in herbem Kontrast zueinander. Wenn Edinburgh schön ist, dann ist Glasgow hart, rau, direkt und liebenswert – wie der hier gesprochene, gewöhnungsbedürftige Akzent.

Nördlich einer Linie, die ungefähr vom Südende des Loch Lomond nach Aberdeen verläuft und bei den Geologen als „Highland Boundary Fault" bekannt ist, beginnen die schottischen Highlands, das Land der Bens (Berge), Glens (Täler) und Lochs (Seen bzw. Fjorde). Das Landschaftsbild ist bestimmt von seltsam abgerundeten und oftmals deutlich über tausend Meter hohen Bergrücken und tiefen, fjordartigen Einschnitten, denen man den Jahrtausende währenden Gletscherschliff ansieht. Dazu das zerklüftete, mit Felsen übersäte Heideland der Hochmoore, die sanft rollenden Hügel des Graslandes und Waldstücke in denen urweltlich knorrige Scotish Pines windschief den hier oft wütenden Elementen trotzen. Die Highlands sind das Ziel der meisten Besucher Schottlands und ihre heutige Form erhielten sie während der letzten Eiszeit, als der gesamte

"East-windy, west-endy", windy and snobbish, the Glaswegians call it. Edinburgh may be the capital city, but Glasgow has most of the capital wealth, because goods have always been produced in Glasgow, and Edinburgh has always been merely a consumer. Glasgow's slums and factories stand in the middle of the inner city, not far from the banks of the Clyde, in a starkly contrasting chessboard pattern. If Edinburgh is beautiful, Glasgow is hard, rough, direct, yet lovable – like the accent spoken here, which takes a great deal of getting used to.

The Scottish Highlands, the land of the bens (mountains), glens (valleys) and lochs (lakes or fjords) begin to the north of a line running approximately from the southern end of Loch Lomond to Aberdeen, and which is known by geologists as the "Highland boundary fault". The landscape is characterised by strangely rounded mountain ridges often well over 3,000 ft. in height and deep, fjord-like clefts testifying to the work of the glaciers over thousands of years, surrounded by the rugged, boulder-strewn heathland of the highland moors, the gently rolling hills of the grassland, and the patches of forest, in which ancient and knotty Scottish Pines withstand the often raging elements. The Highlands are the destination of most visitors to Scotland, and they took on their current form during the last Ice Age, when the whole northern part of the British Isles was buried beneath a thick sheet of ice. Glaciers ground out U-shaped valleys in the mountains, while wind and weather modelled the highland peaks of ancient stone. When the ice melted away, the land rose and water penetrated into the previously ice-filled depres-

l'UNESCO, avec la ville nouvelle néo-classique la plus grande d'Europe. Aujourd'hui, Edimbourg, aux pieds du piton de lave de l'Arthur's Seat, est définitivement devenue un rêve architectural. Battue par les vents et snobinarde, « East-windy and west-endy » comme l'appellent les habitants de Glasgow. Edimbourg est certes la capitale du pays mais Glasgow en détient le capital, car depuis toujours, on consomme à Edimbourg ce qui est produit à Glasgow. Les bidonvilles de Glasgow et les usines contrastent âprement au cœur de la ville, pas loin de la Clyde, comme sur un échiquier. Si Edimbourg est une belle ville, Glasgow en revanche est dure, rude, directe mais digne d'être aimée – comme l'accent que l'on entend ici et auquel il fait s'habituer.

Au nord d'une ligne s'étirant approximativement de l'extrémité sud du Loch Lomond à Aberdeen et à proximité de ce que les géologues appellent la « Highland Boundary Fault », commencent les Highlands écossais, le pays des Bens (montagnes), des Glens (vallées) et des Lochs (lacs ou fjords). Le paysage est dominé par des croupes montagneuses bizarrement arrondies et s'élevant souvent à plus de mille mètres d'altitude et par de profonds sillons, pareils à des fjords, qui révèlent l'érosion continue des glaciers pendant des milliers d'années. Sans oublier les landes crevassées et parsemées de rochers des tourbières de montagne, les collines doucement vallonnées des pâturages et les bois dans lesquels des pins écossais noueux et primitifs, tous penchés, font face aux éléments souvent déchaînés ici. Les Highlands, l'une des principales destinations des touristes visitant l'Ecosse, ont acquis leur forme

que el valle del que se hace mención sólo abarca una quinta parte del país, en él viven casi tres cuartas partes de la población total. Aquí se encuentran los dos grandes núcleos urbanos del país: Glasgow y Edinburgh, dos metrópolis que no podrían ser más diferentes. Edinburgh es –con su centro antiguo histórico, su palacio y su castillo– una bella capital que ha sido declarada patrimonio cultural de la humanidad por la UNESCO y que además tiene la suerte de contar con el mayor ensanche histórico de Europa –la "ciudad nueva"– construido completamente en estilo clasicista. Estas características han convertido a esta urbe ubicada al pie de la silla de Arturo –el antiguo volcán "Arthur's Seat"– en un sublime sueño arquitectónico. Por eso los habitantes de Glasgow dicen de Edinburgh que es "east--windy, west--endy", es decir, pícara y orgullosa. Y añaden que quizá Edinburgh sea la capital, pero Glasgow tiene el capital, pues desde siempre Glasgow fue un centro productivo de mercancías mientras que Edinburgh sólo consume. Los barrios proletarios y las fábricas de Glasgow se encuentran dispuestas en un plano ajedrezado en medio del centro urbano, no lejos del "Clyde", y forman un fuerte contraste entre sí. Si Edinburgh es bella, Glasgow se gana el afecto del viajero con su espíritu duro, áspero y directo; como el dialecto local.

Al norte de una frontera imaginaria cuyo trazado comienza aproximadamente en el extremo sur del Loch Lomond y discurre hacia Aberdeen y que los geólogos llaman la "Highland Boundary Fault", comienzan las Tierras Altas escocesas, la tierra de los "bens" (montañas), "glens" (valles) y "lochs" (lagos y rías). El panorama está dominado por crestas montañosas extrañamente redondeadas y que a

un "sogno" architettonico. „East-windy, west-endy", gli abitanti di Glasgow la definiscono ventosa e snob. Edimburgo sarà "Capital", capitale, ma è Glasgow ad avere il capitale: da sempre le merci vengono prodotte a Glasgow; a Edimburgo vengono solo consumate. Gli slum e le fabbriche di Glasgow, in aspro contrasto l'una con l'altra, sorgono nel cuore del centro storico, poco lontano dal Clyde, e formano una sorta di territorio a scacchiera. Edimburgo è tanto bella quanto Glasgow è dura, rude, diretta e amabile, proprio come il suo particolare accento. A nord della linea immaginaria che collega il lato meridionale del Loch Lomond a Aberdeen si estendono le Highlands scozzesi, definite dai geologi „Highland Boundary Fault": questo è il territorio dei Bens (monti), Glens (valli) e Lochs (laghi o fiordi). Il paesaggio è contraddistinto da dorsi di montagne curiosamente arrotondati, che superano spesso i mille metri, e profonde incisioni, simili a fiordi, che testimoniano l'opera di erosione millenaria dei ghiacciai. E poi dalla brughiera delle torbiere alte, frastagliata e cosparsa di rocce, dalle dolci colline tonde delle praterie, dai tratti di bosco, in cui gli Scotish Pines, nodosi e primitivi, sfidano, contorti dal vento, gli elementi atmosferici, qui spesso violenti. Le Highlands, meta della maggior parte dei turisti che visitano la Scozia, si sono formate nel corso dell'ultima epoca glaciale, quando tutto il nord della Gran Bretagna era seppellito sotto una spessa coltre di ghiaccio. I ghiacciai incisero nella montagna valli a forma di U, il vento e gli agenti atmosferici modellarono nella roccia antica le vette delle Highlands. Dopo lo scioglimento dei ghiacci la terra si sollevò e l'acqua penetrò

Norden Großbritanniens unter einer dicken Eisdecke begraben war. Gletscher hobelten U-förmige Täler in das Gebirge, Wind und Wetter modellierten die Highlandgipfel aus uraltem Gestein. Nach dem Abschmelzen des Eises hob sich das Land und Wasser drang in die zuvor eisgefüllten Senken ein. Eines der markantesten Täler, das sogenannte „Great Glen“ zwischen Fort William und Inverness, unterteilt die Highlands dabei nochmals in die Grampian Mountains im Südosten und die North-West-Highlands. In den Grampians ragen die höchsten Berge ganz Großbritanniens auf, der Ben Nevis (1 344 Meter) und der Ben Macdui (1 312 Meter). Beide Gipfel sind sogenannte Munros, also Berge über 3 000 Fuß (914 Meter im kontinentalen Maß). Ihren Ursprung hat diese merkwürdige Bezeichnung in Sir Henry Munro, einem der Gründungsväter des Scottish Mountaineering Council (SMC), dem schottischen Bergsteigerverband. Von 1894 bis 1897 bekleidete er das Amt des Präsidenten. Er nutzte diese Zeit, um alle Berge die das magische Maß von 3 000 Fuß überragten zu erfassen und in einem dreißigbändigen Werk zu veröffentlichen. Dieser heute „Munro's Tables“ genannte Katalog war für die damalige Zeit revolutionär, da man noch 1890 davon ausging, dass Schottland nicht mehr als 30 Berge dieser Kategorie besaß. Er führte jedoch 277 von ihnen auf und legte damit den Grundstein zur heute beliebtesten Outdoorsportart Großbritanniens, dem Munro Bagging. Dabei geht es um das Besteigen möglichst vieler dieser schottischen Dreitausender.

Im Nordosten der Grampians findet sich das Kerngebiet der Whisky-Herstellung – Speyside genannt. In nahezu

sions. One of the most breathtaking valleys, the so-called "Great Glen" between Fort William and Inverness, divides the Highlands again into the Grampian Mountains in the south-east and the north-west Highlands. The Grampians contain the highest mountains in all of Great Britain, Ben Nevis (4,409 ft.) and Ben Macdui (4,304 ft.). Both peaks are so-called Munros, i.e. mountains over 3,000 ft. (914 metres in continental units). This unusual designation originates from Sir Henry Munro, one of the founding fathers of the Scottish Mountaineering Council (SMC), and its President from 1894 to 1897. He used this time to record all the mountains which exceeded the magic figure of 3,000 ft., publishing his findings in a work of 30 volumes. Known today as "Munro's Tables", this catalogue was at the time revolutionary, since it was still thought in 1890 that Scotland had no more than 30 peaks in this category. Sir Henry however listed 277 of them, thereby laying the cornerstone for the most popular outdoor sport of Great Britain today, Munro Bagging, which consists of climbing as many as possible of these Scottish 3,000-footers.

To the north-east of the Grampians lies the heart of the whisky-producing area – called Speyside. Almost every village is home to one of the over 130 distilleries with their typical pagoda roofs, under which the water of life, as whisky is known in Gaelic, is produced and stored according to ancient and secret recipes. Only two distilling vats are used, and whisky is of course spelled here with only a "y" at the end, as opposed to "whiskey", which comes from Ireland.

actuelle au cours des dernières glaciations lorsque tout le nord de la Grande-Bretagne était enseveli sous une épaisse couche de glace. Les glaciers ont creusé des vallées en forme de U dans les montagnes, le vent et les intempéries ont modelé les sommets de roches très anciennes des Highlands. Après la fonte des glaces, le sol s'est soulevé et l'eau a pénétré dans les dépressions auparavant remplies de glace. L'une des vallées les plus intéressantes, ladite «Great Glen» entre Fort William et Inverness, découpe encore une fois les Highlands : les Grampian Mountains au sud-est et les North-West-Highlands. Les Grampians s'enorgueillissent de posséder les plus hautes montagnes de toute la Grande-Bretagne, le Ben Nevis (1 344 m) et le Ben Macdui (1 312 m). Ces deux sommets sont ce que l'on appelle des Munros, c'est-à-dire des montagnes de plus de 3 000 pieds (914 m dans notre système métrique). Elles doivent cette appellation bizarre à Sir Henry Munro, l'un des fondateurs du Scottish Mountaineering Council (SMC), fédération d'alpinisme écossaise, dont il a été le président de 1894 à 1897. Il a mis à profit cette période pour recenser toutes les montagnes dépassant le seuil magique des 3 000 pieds et les publier dans une série de trois tomes. Ce catalogue appelé «Munro's Tables» était un ouvrage révolutionnaire pour l'époque car on était persuadé en 1890 encore que l'Ecosse ne possédait pas plus de trente montagnes de cette catégorie. Il en recense toutefois 277 et pose ainsi la première pierre du sport national de plein air numéro un en Grande-Bretagne, le Munro Bagging qui consiste à gravir un nombre maximum de ces montagnes de plus de trois mille pieds.

menudo superan los mil metros así como por profundas gargantas similares a rías en las que se aprecia claramente la erosión que produjo la milenaria presencia de glaciares. A todo esto se une el escabroso paisaje de landas salpicadas de formaciones rocosas que se puede admirar en la zona de los pantanos altos, las suaves colinas de las praderas así como bosques en los que los nudosos pinos escoceses plantan cara al viento y a los a menudo furiosos elementos. Las Tierras Altas, que son el objetivo de la mayoría de los visitantes de Escocia, adquirieron su actual aspecto durante la última era glacial en la que todo el norte de Gran Bretaña se encontraba cubierto por una gruesa capa de hielo. Mientras que los glaciares horadaban valles en forma de U entre las sierras, el viento y la intemperie se encargaron de cincelar las cumbres en la antiquísima roca de las montañas. Tras el deshielo, el terreno se elevó y las aguas fueron inundando las depresiones que antes estaban cubiertas de hielo. El "Great Glen", uno de los más impresionantes valles, se extiende entre Fort William e Inverness y subdivide a las Tierras Altas entre los Montes Grampianos al sudeste y las Tierras Altas del noroeste. En la Cordillera de los Grampianos se elevan las más altas montañas de toda Gran Bretaña: el Ben Nevis (1.344 metros) y el Ben Macdui (1.312 metros). Ambas cumbres son "Munros", es decir montañas que superan los 3000 pies (914 metros en la medida continental). Esta curiosa denominación tiene su origen en Sir Henry Munro, uno de los fundadores del Scottish Mountaineering Council (SMC), de la asociación de montañeros escoceses de la que fue presidente de 1894 a 1897. Sir Henry aprovechó el periodo de su presidencia para registrar estadísticamente

nelle depressioni, che prima erano riempite di ghiaccio. Una delle valli più caratteristiche, la cosiddetta "Great Glen", situata tra Fort William e Inverness, suddivide ancora una volta le Highlands nei Monti Grampiani, a sud est, e nelle North-West-Highlands. Tra i Monti Grampiani si ergono le montagne più alte dell'intera Gran Bretagna: il Ben Nevis (1.344 metri) e il Ben Macdui (1.312 metri). Le due vette sono cosiddette Munros, ovvero monti che superano i 3.000 piedi (914 metri nell'unità di misura occidentale). Questo nome bizzarro deriva da Sir Henry Munro, uno dei padri fondatori dello Scottish Mountaineering Council (SMC), l'associazione alpinisti scozzesi di cui fu presidente dal 1894 al 1897. Durante il periodo della sua presidenza rilevò le montagne che superavano la magica misura dei 3.000 piedi e le pubblicò in un'opera di trenta volumi. Allora il catalogo, che oggi è chiamato „Munro's Tables", era rivoluzionario. Nel 1890, infatti, si presupponeva che la Scozia non avesse più di 30 montagne con queste caratteristiche. Sir Munro ne enumerò 277, gettando le fondamenta dello sport outdoor oggi più amato in Gran Bretagna: il *Munro Bagging*, che consiste nello scalare il numero maggiore di monti scozzesi che superano i tremila.

A nord-est dei Monti Grampiani si trova lo Speyside, la regione più importante per la produzione di whisky. Le oltre 130 distillerie dai tipici tetti a pagoda sotto i quali sulla base di ricette segrete si produce e immagazzina l'acqua della vita (così viene chiamato il whisky in gaelico) sono distribuite in quasi ogni paese. Per la sua produzione si impiegano solo due alambicchi e naturalmente, qui, whisky si scrive esclusivamente con la „y" in fondo.

jedem Dorf findet sich eine der über 130 Brennereien mit ihren typischen Pagodendächern, unter denen das Wasser des Lebens, wie Whisky auf Gälisch genannt wird, nach geheimen Rezepturen hergestellt und gelagert wird. Es werden nur zwei Brennblasen benutzt und Whisky wird hier selbstverständlich nur mit „y" am Ende geschrieben.
Im Nordwesten Schottlands wird das Landschaftsbild dann äußerst dramatisch. Nur selten begegnet man hier anderen Menschen und in der weiten, durch riesige Moorflächen geprägten Gegend blinken tausende von kleinen und großen Seen. Darüber wölbt sich eine Himmelskuppel, die klarer als sonst irgendwo zu sein scheint. Schnell wechseln hier die Lichtstimmungen, von düster und bedrohlich über melancholisch bedrückend bis zur frohlockenden Heiterkeit schwankt das gefühlte Barometer, manchmal innerhalb weniger Stunden. Die skurril geformten und vereinzelt aufragenden Berge wirken wie stumme Zeugen aus einer anderen Welt. Was geologisch gesehen auch gar nicht so verkehrt ist, denn die hier anzutreffenden Gesteine gehören zu den ältesten der Welt. Knapp drei Milliarden Jahre ist der Untergrund alt, da ist der ein oder andere Kratzer an der Oberfläche kaum verwunderlich. Den Bergen vorgelagert ist im Westen und Norden Schottlands eine reizvolle Küste. Mehrere Fjorde dringen bis weit in das Hinterland ein und sorgen für eine enge Verzahnung zwischen Meer und Land. Malerische Strände liegen versteckt in verschlungenen Buchten, landeinwärts wechseln sich glitzernde Seen mit tosenden Flüssen ab, die sie sich durch enge Schluchten schlängeln. Obwohl die Natur hier die tonangebende Gewalt ist, hat der Mensch durchaus seine Spuren in dieser

In the north-west of Scotland, the landscape becomes truly dramatic. Only rarely does one come across another living soul in this region of broad moorland areas, where thousands of lakes large and small glitter in the fleeting sunlight. Above arches the dome of the sky which seems to be clearer than anywhere else on earth. The lighting changes quickly here, from murky and threatening, to melancholy and oppressive and back to triumphant sunshine, a veritable barometer of moods, sometimes all within a few hours. The strangely-shaped, isolated peaks rising up here and there stand mute witnesses from another world – which is not at all unusual from a geological point of view, because some of the rock found here is amongst the oldest in the world. The bedrock is around 3 billion years old, so that a scratch or two on the surface is hardly surprising. The mountains are bordered in the west and north by a fascinating coastline. Several fjords penetrate far into the hinterland, creating a landscape alternating continually between land and sea. Picturesque beaches lie concealed in sheltered bays, while inland, sparkling lakes alternate with torrential rivers which wind their way through narrow gorges. Although nature here is the dominating force, man has certainly also left his mark on the landscape. Almost everywhere one can find picturesque villages, small fishing ports or even just one of the many isolated, squat-looking, universally whitewashed cottages nestling amongst the grandiose natural backdrop of hills and moors. Particularly imposing are the castles such as Duart Castle on Mull, or the most famous castle in Scotland, Eilean Donan Castle on Loch Duich. Built on the border

Le centre de la fabrication du whisky – Speyside – se trouve au nord-est des Grampians. Presque chaque village possède sa propre distillerie (plus de 130 au total) avec son toit typique en forme de pagode sous lequel l'eau de vie, autre nom du whisky en gaélique, est fabriquée selon des formules secrètes puis stocké. On utilise uniquement deux alambics et le mot whisky s'écrit ici bien sûr ici «ky» à la fin et non «key» comme en Irlande par exemple.
Dans le nord-ouest de l'Ecosse, le paysage revêt un caractère dramatique. Il est rare de rencontrer ici âme qui vive mais des milliers de lacs, petits et grands, scintillent dans cette immensité dominée par des étendues marécageuses avec, au-dessus, un dôme céleste qui semble plus clair que partout ailleurs. La lumière change vite ici, elle peut être lugubre et menaçante mais aussi déprimante et mélancolique ou encore exubérante et gaie, en l'espace de quelques heures seulement. Ces montagnes aux formes bizarroïdes et parfois très élevées, semblent être des témoins muets d'un autre monde. Ce qui, d'un point de vue géologique n'est pas aussi faux qu'on pourrait le croire, car les roches que l'on trouve ici comptent parmi les plus anciennes de notre planète. Le sol ici a environ trois milliards d'années et les quelques rayures à la surface ne sont donc guère surprenantes. Dans l'ouest et le nord de l'Ecosse, les montagnes sont bordées par un magnifique littoral côtier. Plusieurs fjords s'insinuent loin dans les terres, créant un relief dentelé entre terre et mer. Des plages pittoresques se dissimulent dans des anses entrelacées, vers l'intérieur des terres, des lacs scintillants alternent avec des rivières mugissantes qui sinuent à travers d'étroites gorges. Bien que la nature donne ici le ton,

todos los montes que superaban ese límite mágico de los 3000 pies y publicar sus resultados en una obra de tres tomos. Ese catálogo –que hoy se denomina las tablas de Munro, "Munro's Tables"– era revolucionario para su época, ya que todavía en 1890 se suponía que Escocia no poseía más de 30 montañas de esa categoría. Sir Henry sin embargo registró 277 de ellos y fundó de esta forma el deporte de tiempo libre más popular actualmente en Gran Bretaña, el "Munro Bagging". Se trata simplemente de escalar el mayor número posible de esos "tres mil" escoceses.
En el nordeste de los Montes Grampianos se encuentra la „Speyside", la cuna de la producción del whisky. En prácticamente cada pueblo hay alguna de las más de 130 destilerías con sus típicos techos que recuerdan a las pagodas. Allí se produce y almacena siguiendo recetas secretas el "agua de la vida", como se denomina al whisky en gaélico. Sólo se emplean dos pipas de destilación y naturalmente aquí la palabra "whisky" sólo se escribe con "y" al final.
En el noroeste de Escocia el paisaje adquiere su máximo dramatismo. Resulta raro encontrar gente en estos amplios parajes caracterizados por enormes superficies pantanosas en los que parpadea el brillo de miles de pequeños y grandes lagos. Y todo ello bajo una cúpula celeste que aquí parece más clara que en ninguna otra parte. Aquí la luz hace cambiar rápidamente los ambientes: de oscuro y amenazante a claro y alegre pasando por melancólico y opresivo. A veces en tan sólo horas. Las montañas que destacan individualmente con sus extravagantes formas parecen ser testigos mudos de otro mundo. Lo que, por cierto, no es tan falso desde un punto de vista geológico, ya que las rocas que aquí

A nord-ovest si estende un paesaggio estremamente suggestivo in cui raramente ci si imbatte in altre persone. In questa regione ampia, contraddistinta da enormi superfici paludose, scintillano migliaia di laghi, piccoli e grandi. In alto si inarca la cupola celeste che qui sembra essere più limpida che altrove. Gli effetti della luce si alternano rapidamente: da cupo e minaccioso, a soffocante e malinconico, a esultante e allegro, il barometro "delle sensazioni" muta nell'arco di solo qualche ora. I monti, dalla forma bizzarra, emergono sporadici, muti testimoni di un altro mondo. Dal punto di vista geologico questo paesaggio non è poi così assurdo. Questa la roccia é una delle più antiche al mondo. Il sottosuolo ha quasi tre miliardi di anni: non c'è da sorprendersi, quindi, se sulla sua superficie si aprono qua e là delle crepe. Davanti alle montagne, a ovest e a nord della Scozia, si estende una costa affascinante. I numerosi fiordi penetrano in profondità nell'entroterra unendo tra loro terra e mare. Spiagge pittoresche trovano riparo in insenature tortuose. Verso l'interno del paese laghi luccicanti si alternano a fiumi mugghianti che serpeggiano attraverso strette gole. Nonostante la natura sia l'elemento predominante, l'uomo ha lasciato tracce nel paesaggio. Ovunque sorgono paesi pittoreschi, piccoli porti di pescatori o anche solo una delle numerose casette intonacate di bianco, immerse nel cuore di una grandiosa cornice naturale. Le fortificazioni come il Duart Castle sull'isola di Mull, oppure il castello più famoso della Scozia, l'Eilean Donan Castle presso Loch Duich, risaltano in tutta la loro imponenza. Costruite al confine tra mare e monti sembrano ergersi nel punto d'incontro tra la natura e l' uomo.

Landschaft hinterlassen. Nahezu überall findet man pittoreske Dörfer, kleine Fischereihäfen oder auch nur eines der vielen gedrungen wirkenden und allesamt weiß getünchten Häuschen inmitten einer grandiosen Naturkulisse. Besonders imposant wirken Trutzbauten wie das Duart Castle auf Mull oder die berühmteste Burg Schottlands, das Eilean Donan Castle am Loch Duich. Errichtet an den Grenzen zwischen Meer und Gebirge scheinen sie zwischen Natur und Mensch zu stehen.

Von den insgesamt 787 schottischen Inseln sind nur 130 von Menschen bewohnt. Inseln wie Staffa, die Mendelssohn in der Hebriden-Ouvertüre vertont hat, oder Skye gehören zum schönsten, was Schottland zu bieten hat. Raue Küstenlandschaften liegen direkt neben hochalpin anmutenden Bergketten, unergründlich tiefe Moorseen grenzen an Buchten mit weißen Sandstränden, deren türkisgrüne Wässer an die Karibik erinnern. Allerdings wird man von den Temperaturen schnell eines Besseren belehrt. Denn bei aller Romantik: In Schottland ist es häufig kalt und nass. Aber das gehört dazu, zu Schottland, der Bühne eines manchmal unwirklich schönen, oft menschenleeren Landes, bespielt von Sonne, Wolken, Regenschauern und Wind.

between sea and mountains, they seem to stand somewhere between nature and man.

Of the total of 787 Scottish islands, only 130 are inhabited by people. Islands such as Staffa, set to music by Mendelssohn in the Hebrides Overture, or Skye, are amongst the most beautiful sights that Scotland has to offer. Rugged coastal landscapes extend directly beside mountain chains as if from the high alps, unfathomly deep moorland lakes adjoin bays fringed by white sand beaches, whose turquoise-green water reminds the observer of the Caribbean, although one is quickly disabused of this notion by the prevailing temperatures, for despite all the romanticism, the weather in Scotland is frequently cold and wet. But this is all part of the package, of Scotland, the stage of a sometimes unbelievably beautiful, often deserted country, bathed in sun, clouds, rain showers and wind.

l'homme a laissé aussi de nombreuses traces bien distinctes dans ce paysage : des villages pittoresques, de petits ports de pêche ou même l'une de ces petites maisons trapues toutes blanchies à la chaux plantées au milieu d'un décor grandiose comme il en existe tant. Les châteaux, pareils à d'imposantes forteressses, comme par exemple le Duart Castle sur l'île de Mull ou le plus célèbre château d'Ecosse, l'Eilean Donan Castle en bordure du Loch Duich, sont particulièrement imposants. Edifié aux frontières entre la mer et les montagnes, ils semblent hésiter entre la nature et l'homme.

Seulement 130 des 787 îles écossaises sont habitées. L'Ile de Staffa, mise en musique par Mendelssohn dans l'ouverture des «Hybrides», ou l'Ile de Skye par exemple sont quelques-uns des joyaux que possède l'Ecosse. Des paysages côtiers sauvages jouxtent directement des chaînes de montagne très élevées, des lacs tourbeux aux profondeurs insondables bordent des baies avec des plages de sable blanc dont les eaux vert turquoise rappellent les Caraïbes, mais on est rapidement détrompé par les températures. Car quoi que très romantique, l'Ecosse est un pays souvent froid et humide. Mais c'est tout ça l'Ecosse, un pays à la beauté parfois irréelle, souvent désert, où jouent le soleil, les nuages, les ondées et le vent.

se pueden encontrar se cuentan entre las más antiguas del mundo. Si se tiene en cuenta que el subsuelo tiene aquí una antigüedad de casi tres mil millones de años, no resultarán sorprendentes las huellas de la erosión que se aprecien en la superficie. Tanto al norte como al oeste de Escocia se extiende frente a las montañas una fascinante costa. Varias rías penetran profundamente en el interior produciendo así esa singular imbricación que se aprecia aquí entre el mar y el paisaje. Escondidas en las enrevesadas bahías se pueden encontrar pintorescas calas. Hacia el interior se relevan brillantes lagos con ruidosos ríos que fluyen a través de estrechas gargantas.

De las 787 islas escocesas sólo 130 están habitadas. Algunas islas como la de Staffa, en la que se inspiró Mendelssohn al escribir la obertura Las Hébridas o la de Skye son de lo más bello que puede ofrecer Escocia. Directamente junto a escabrosos litorales se alzan sierras de aspecto alpino; lagos pantanosos de indeterminada profundidad limitan con bahías que albergan playas de arenas blancas cuyas aguas de color turquesa nos hacen pensar en el Caribe. Pero ésta es sólo una impresión pasajera, ya que las temperaturas reinantes nos recordarán en seguida donde estamos y, a pesar de todo el romanticismo, la verdad es que en Escocia a menudo el tiempo es húmedo y frío. Pero así es Escocia, ese país de belleza a veces irreal que a menudo parece casi despoblado. El país que el sol, las nubes, los chubascos y el viento han elegido para escenificar sus juegos.

Solo 130 delle complessive 787 isole scozzesi sono abitate. Isole come Staffa, immortalata da Mendelssohn nell'Ouverture "Le Ebridi", o Skye, sono quanto di meglio la Scozia possa offrire. Paesaggi costieri selvaggi, accanto ad amene catene alpine, laghi palustri, profondi e imperscrutabili, rasentano insenature con spiagge di sabbia bianca e acqua color verde turchese, simile a quella caraibica. Ma basta uno sguardo alle temperature per tornare rapidamente alla realtà. Romanticismo a parte, la Scozia è spesso fredda e piovosa. Fa parte del gioco, fa parte della Scozia, fa parte di uno spettacolo interpretato da sole, nuvole, scrosci di pioggia e vento la cui scenografia, spesso solitaria, è talvolta di una bellezza tale da sembrare irreale.

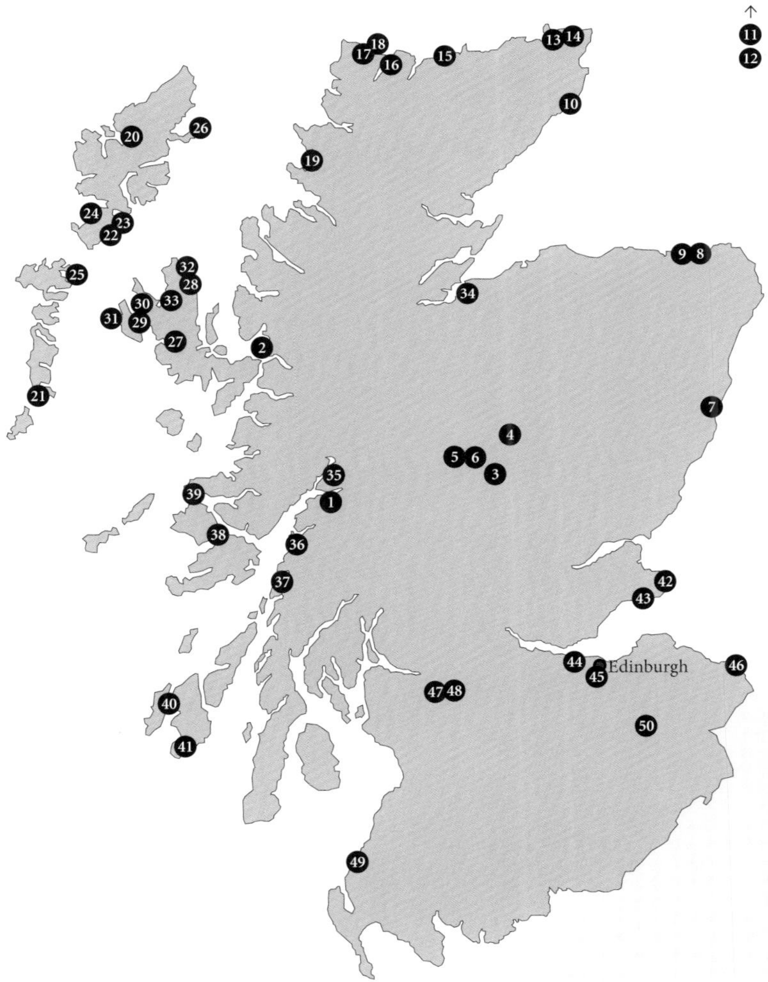

11
12
13
14
17
18
16
15
10
20
26
19
24
23
22
9
8
32
25
28
34
30
33
31
29
27
2
21
7
4
5
6
3
35
39
1
38
36
37
42
43
44
Edinburgh
45
46
47
48
40
50
41
49

1 Loch Leven, Grampian Mountains, West Highlands

2 Eilean Donan Castle, Loch Duich, Northwest Highlands

► 3 Queens View, Loch Tummel, Grampian Mountains, Highlands

4 Glen Shee, Grampian Mountains

5 Glen Garry, Atholl, Grampian Mountains

► 6 Blair Castle, Atholl, Grampian Mountains

7 Dunnottar Castle, East Coast

8 Crovie, Northeast Coast

► 9 Crovie, Northeast Coast

10 Lybster Harbour, Northeast Coast

11 Eshaness, West Coast, Shetland Islands

12 Eshaness, West Coast, Shetland Islands

► **13** Dunnet Head Lighthouse, Pentland Firth, North Coast

14 Dunnet Head Lighthouse, Pentland Firth, North Coast

► **15** Torrisdale Beach, North Coast

16 Loch Eriboll, North Coast

17 Durness, North Coast

18 Durness, North Coast

19 Loch Kirkaig, Inverpolly Nature Reservation, West Coast

► 20 Calanais, Standing Stones, Isle of Lewis, Outer Hebrides

21 Sound of Eriskay, South Uist, Western Isles

22 Plocrapool, Harris, Western Isles, Outer Hebrides

23 Plocrapool Point, Harris, Western Isles, Outer Hebrides

24 Luskentyre, Harris, Western Isles, Outer Hebrides

► **25** Loch Maddy, North Uist, Western Isles, Outer Hebrides

S.Y.106

26 Tiumpan Head Lighthouse, Isle of Lewis, Outer Hebrides

27 Loch Bracadale, Isle of Skye, Inner Hebrides

28 Quiraing, Isle of Skye, Inner Hebrides

29 Colbost, Loch Dunvegan, Isle of Skye, Inner Hebrides

30 Dunvegan Castle, Isle of Skye, Inner Hebrides

► 31 Neist Point, Isle of Skye, Inner Hebrides

32 Trotternish, Isle of Skye, Inner Hebrides

33 Trotternish, Isle of Skye, Inner Hebrides

► **34** Urquhart Castle, Loch Ness, Highlands

35 Loch Leven, Grampian Mountains, West Highlands

36 Castle Stalker, Loch Linnhe, West Highlands

37 Sound of Kerrera, Oban, West Coast

38 Sound of Mull, Isle of Mull, Inner Hebrides

39 Tobermory, Isle of Mull, Inner Hebrides

► **40** Loch Indaal, Islay, Inner Hebrides

41 Laphroaig Distillery, Islay, Inner Hebrides

► **42** Crail, Fife, East Coast

KY992

KY449

43 Anstruther, Fife, East Coast

44 South Queensferry, Forth Bridges, Firth of Forth

45 Edinburgh Castle, Edinburgh

46 St. Abb's Head, The Borders, Southeast Coast

▸ **47** Armadillo, River Clyde, Glasgow

CLYDEPORT
Bells Bridge

 River Clyde, Glasgow

49 Black Head Lighthouse, Galloway, The Borders, Southwest Coast

► **50** Scott's View, Eildon Hills, The Borders

AXEL M. MOSLER wurde 1953 in Dortmund geboren, wo er auch sein Fachhochschulstudium der Photographie absolvierte. Seit 1977 ist er als freier Photo-Designer und Landschaftsphotograph tätig. Panoramaphotographie ist fester Bestandteil seiner photographischen Arbeit, die nicht nur in zahlreichen Bildbänden renommierter Verlage vorliegt, sondern auch auf vielen Ausstellungen im In- und Ausland gezeigt wird. Ausgedehnte Photoreisen haben ihn unter anderem nach Schottland, Norwegen, Kanada, Griechenland und in die Toskana geführt.

RALF GANTZHORN, geboren 1964 in Eutin (Ostholstein), lebt und arbeitet als freier Journalist und Geologe in Hamburg. Neben Patagonien gehört Schottland zu den Reisezielen, zu denen er immer wieder und zu allen Jahreszeiten zurückkehrt. Ursache für die langjährige Begeisterung ist ein einjähriger Studienaufenthalt an der Universität von Aberdeen, der ihm Gelegenheit gab, Land und Leute ausgiebig kennen zu lernen. Besonders nachhaltig in Erinnerung geblieben sind ihm dabei die Inseln der Inneren und Äußeren Hebriden, auf denen er neben zahlreichen Wander- und Trekkingtouren auch Erstbegehungen im senkrechten Fels unternahm.

AXEL M. MOSLER was born in 1953 in Dortmund, where he also graduated from his photographic studies at the technical high school. Since 1977 he has been active as a freelance photo-designer and landscape photographer. Panorama photography is a permanent feature of his photographic work which is not only available in many illustrated volumes from renowned publishers, but is also presented at many exhibitions at home and abroad. Extensive photographic expeditions have taken him to Scotland, Norway, Canada, Greece and Tuscany among others.

RALF GANTZHORN was born in 1964 in Eutin (Ostholstein), and lives and works as a freelance journalist and geologist in Hamburg. In addition to Patagonia, Scotland is one of the travel destinations to which he returns time and again and at all times of the year. His long-standing love of the country originates from a one-year course of study at the University of Aberdeen, which gave him the opportunity to get to know the country and its people at first hand. Especially enshrined in his memory are the islands of the Inner and Outer Hebrides, where in addition to many walking and trekking tours, he made his first encounters with vertical rock faces.

AXEL M. MOSLER est né en 1953 à Dortmund, où il a fait des études supérieures de photographie. Depuis 1977 il travaille comme photo-designer indépendant et photographe paysager. Les panoramas qu'il photographie régulièrement ne sont pas seulement présentés dans les nombreux livres de photographies d'éditeurs réputés mais aussi dans de nombreuses expositions nationales et internationales. Les longs voyages entrepris dans le cadre de son travail l'ont conduit entre autres en Ecosse, en Norvège, au Canada, en Grèce et en Toscane.

RALF GANTZHORN, né en 1964 à Eutin (Ostholstein), vit à Hambourg où il travaille comme journaliste indépendant et géologue. L'Ecosse, tout comme la Patagonie, est l'une de ses destinations de voyage favorites où il se rend régulièrement et à n'importe quelle saison. Il n'a cessé de s'intéresser à ce pays depuis qu'il a passé une année à l'université d'Aberdeen, au cours de laquelle il a découvert l'Ecosse et ses habitants. Il garde notamment des souvenirs vivaces des Iles des Hébrides intérieures et extérieures où il a fait de nombreuses randonnées ainsi que l'ascension de plusieurs parois verticales.

AXEL M. MOSLER nació en Dortmund en1953, donde también realizó sus estudios de fotografía en la Universidad de Ciencias Aplicadas. Desde 1977 trabaja como diseñador fotográfico libre y fotógrafo paisajístico. La fotografía panorámica es parte esencial de su trabajo. Estas imágenes no sólo pueden apreciarse en un gran número de volúmenes publicados por casas editoriales de prestigio, sino también en muchas exposiciones tanto del país como del extranjero. Largos y extensos viajes fotográficos lo han llevado, entre otros lugares, a Escocia, Noruega, Canadá, Grecia y la Toscana.

RALF GANTZHORN, nació en 1964 en Eutin (Ostholstein, Alemania). Vive y trabaja de periodista libre y geólogo en Hamburgo. Entre los destinos a los que siempre regresa en todas las estaciones del año se encuentran Escocia y Patagonia. El origen de su pasión de muchos años ya por Escocia se encuentra en una estancia de estudios de un año de duración en la Universidad de Aberdeen. Esa estancia le brindó la oportunidad de conocer a fondo el país y sus gentes. Entre los paisajes que más profundamente quedaron grabados en su memoria se encuentran las Islas Hébridas exteriores e interiores en las cuales, además de numerosas expediciones de senderismo y ciclismo de montaña, también realizó primeras escaladas sobre roca vertical.

AXEL M. MOSLER è nato nel 1953 a Dortmund, dove si è laureato in tecnica fotografica. Dal 1977 è attivo come designer fotografico e fotografo di paesaggi. La foto panoramica è parte essenziale del suo lavoro che, oltre ad essere pubblicato in numerosi libri di fotografia per rinomati editori, è stato esposto in molte mostre tenutesi in Germania e in altri paesi. I suoi articolati viaggi fotografici lo hanno condotto tra l'altro in Scozia, Norvegia, Canada, Grecia e Toscana.

<

RALF GANTZHORN è nato nel 1964 a Eutin (Ostholstein) e vive ad Amburgo, dove lavora come giornalista free-lance e geologo. La Scozia, assieme alla Patagonia, è una delle mete di viaggio che visita più spesso, in ogni stagione. La sua passione per il paese risale a parecchio tempo fa ed à nata in occasione di un soggiorno di studio annuale presso l'Università di Aberdeen, che gli offrì l'opportunità di conoscere approfonditamente il paese e i suoi abitanti. Sulle isole Ebridi Interne e Esterne, che si sono impresse nella sua memoria in modo quasi indelebile, ha effettuato numerose escursioni e trekking, nonché le prime spedizioni su roccia perpendicolare.

ISBN: 978-3-89823-348-4

Concept: Bernhard Wipfler, Sebastian Wipfler, Marcus Bela Schmitt
Design: Designgruppe Fanz & Neumayer | Marcus Bela Schmitt & EDITION PANORAMA | Diana May
Editorial department: Dr. Michael Barchet, Wolfgang Roth
Translations: Global-Text Fachübersetzungen Heidelberg | Mark Woolfe, Jocelyne Abarca, Dr. Maria Carasi, Sebastián González Mohíno
Printing: abcdruck GmbH, Heidelberg
Bookbinding: Josef Spinner Großbuchbinderei GmbH, Ottersweier

EDITION PANORAMA GmbH
G7, 14
D-68159 Mannheim

www.editionpanorama.com

A production by EDITION**PANORAMA**

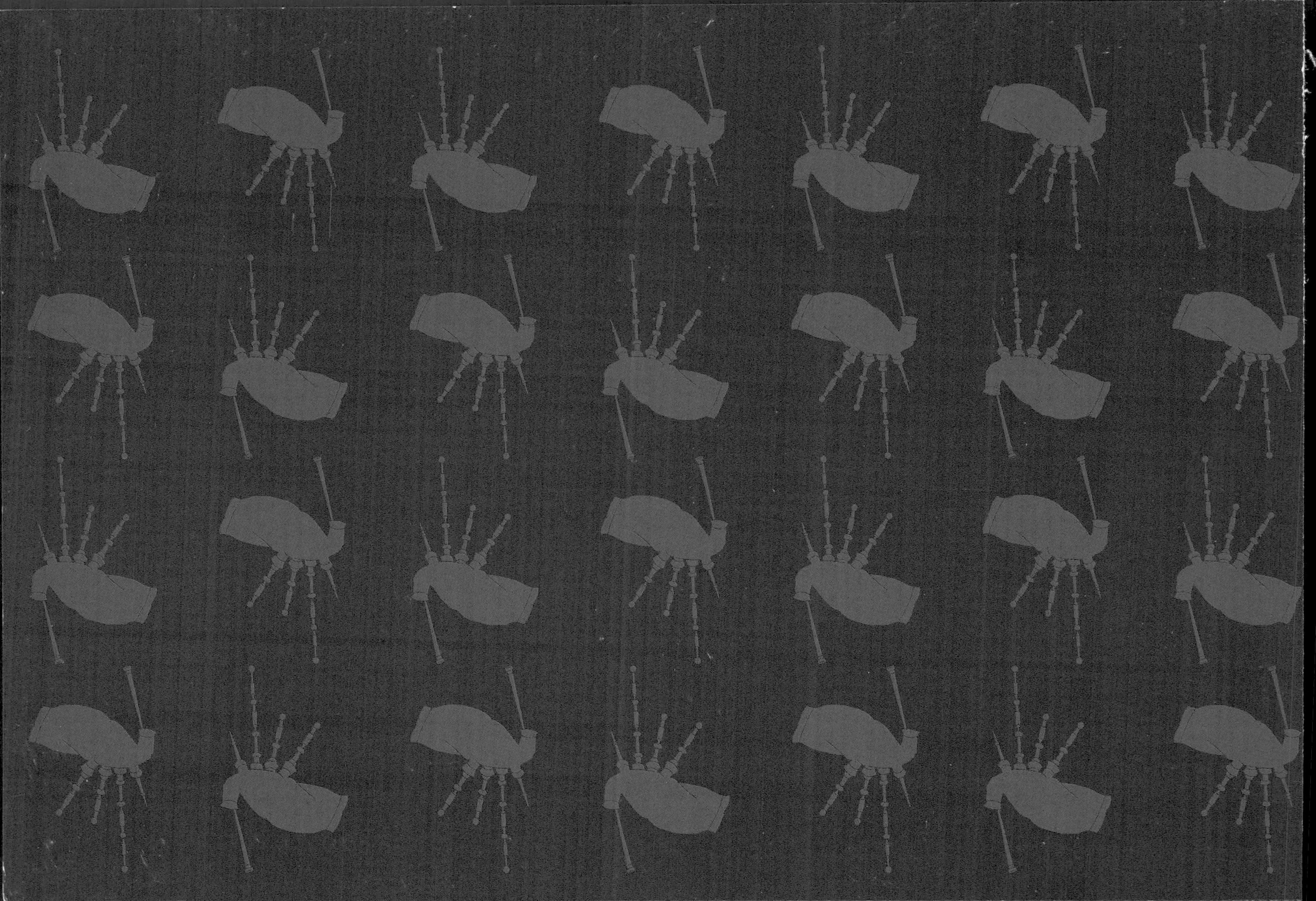